365 QUC ＿ ＿

ACCELERATE YOUR
CAREER AND FIND
BALANCE IN LIFE

James Espey OBE

Cherish
EDITIONS

First published in Great Britain 2022 by Cherish Editions
Cherish Editions is a trading style of Shaw Callaghan Ltd &
Shaw Callaghan 23 USA, INC.
The Foundation Centre
Navigation House, 48 Millgate, Newark
Nottinghamshire NG24 4TS UK
www.triggerhub.org
Text Copyright © 2022 James Espey

British Library Cataloguing in Publication Data
A CIP catalogue record for this book is available upon request
from the British Library
ISBN: 978-1-913615-60-4

This book is also available in the following eBook formats:
ePUB: 978-1-913615-61-1

Cover design by Aimee Coveney
Typeset by Lapiz Digital Services

ENDORSEMENTS FOR JAMES ESPEY OBE

"A unique take on the wisdom of quotes. Entertaining and makes you think!"
Neville Isdell, former global chairman and CEO of The Coca-Cola Company

"James has spent his career observing, thinking and summing things up succinctly. These quotes provide moments to reflect and be guided by someone who has seen around a few of the bends in the road ahead."
Peter Bauer, CEO of Mimecast

"James's ability to draw a quote or a one-liner to sum up a 'situation' – tricky, funny or even just routine – has always been a feature of his management and leadership. This unique, spontaneous communication style provides inspiration to all who deal with him."
Michael Keiller, former CEO of Morrison Bowmore Distillers Ltd

"I am privileged and proud to have known James for more than 60 years. He has always had an excellent grasp on and insight into what it takes to succeed in one's business life. This book is a visionary tribute to his acute observations, and the quotes and his comments provide a timely reminder of how to survive the challenges of our post-pandemic world."
Derek G. Wilson MBE, Chevalier de L'Ordre National du Mérite, president of Andros UK

To my wife and daughters who have inspired and supported me through all the years, and to my six grandchildren who are the future.

CONTENTS

ABOUT THE AUTHOR

I was born in Livingstone, Zambia, in 1943, where my father was a colonial police officer in what was then Northern Rhodesia. Sadly, my parents divorced in 1949 when I was six and, as a result, I was sent to boarding school in Cape Town, four days and four nights away by train, for the next ten and a half years.

I spent some six months of my life on a train and only came home twice a year, often to a different town because we lived in many different parts of the country.

Being one of the poorer kids at school was not easy, but I learned a great deal. First of all, I learned **respect** – sadly, something that's all too often missing in life these days. I learned the importance of **personal values**, such as being on time: "If you are not early, you are late." I also learned that you get nothing without "hard work and perseverance". Boarding school was tough, the teachers were very strict, and punishment including hidings was often given. One had to learn to be totally emotionally reserved and to keep everything to oneself. It was a sign of weakness to show emotion, which of course is not the way today. There was certainly no understanding of mental health when I was young. Fortunately, being reasonably good at sport and reasonably intelligent made a big difference.

On leaving school I did a Bachelor of Commerce degree, mostly part-time because I ran out of money. As a result, I used to work 8:30am to 5pm, go to lectures from 5:30 to 7:30pm four nights a week, with lectures from 9am to midday on a Saturday morning. Two nights a week I was a waiter in a restaurant. One of my favourite quotes now is, "If you want something done, ask a busy person." It gave me ambition and drive. I was going to be a chartered accountant, but I could not afford to be articled, so I switched to marketing, which has been my life ever since.

I started my career in the grocery trade, working for Spar when supermarkets were in their infancy, and it rapidly taught me that "the only real boss in life is the customer" who votes with his or her feet. Everyone else is purely an official or a functionary in the business. In 1968 I borrowed money to do an MBA degree, which gave me a good kick-start into general business. Immediately thereafter, I worked for Coca-Cola and then, in January 1970, joined Gilbey's South Africa as the sales manager and, later, marketing director. Today it is part of what is now Diageo plc, the top global liquor company, with a market valuation above £90 billion and operational profit of about £4 billion – an amazing story in itself, and I was privileged to be involved for 23 years.

In 1977 I was transferred to London to head up global marketing for IDV (International Distillers & Vintners, part of Grand Metropolitan), which at that stage was making somewhere around £10 million per annum. My job was to lead innovation and build Baileys Irish Cream into the world's best-selling liqueur. In the process I did an action-learning Strategic Planning PhD, charting how IDV would make £150 million within ten years. In 1997 Grand Metropolitan and thus IDV merged with Guinness plc to form the mighty Diageo plc. I also spent six years with United Distillers (the spirits arm of Guinness plc) from 1986 to 1992 before taking over as the chief executive of Chivas Bros. Ltd until December 1997.

Looking back at my corporate career, I had much to do with building Baileys into what it is today, but I was also very involved in creating and building Piat D'or wines, Malibu, the Six Classic Malts, and the blended whiskies Johnnie Walker Blue Label and Chivas Regal 18, amongst others. I was actually fired for creating and launching Chivas Regal 18 because the chairman disagreed with me. I stuck to my guns, and today it is the most popular 18-year-old brand in the world. I had the comfort of a good exit contract – which you must always negotiate if you are headhunted, as that is when you are at your strongest. One of my quotes is, "It's not so bad being fired!"

There may come a day when it happens to you. You have to look for opportunity and grab it, but you must also have the courage to stand up for what you truly believe.

At the age of 55, I became a non-executive director sitting on a number of boards and an entrepreneur backing young people. I believe passionately in the future of our youth, and we have to give them encouragement and support. Of course, some of my investments have failed. There are always failures but, "If you never leave the shore, you will never reach the other side," and, "Nothing ventured, nothing gained." On the other hand, I have been delighted to have been involved in some serious successes – in particular, Mimecast, a company protecting business against viral email attacks. It is now valued at $5.8 billion on the US Nasdaq stock market (MIME) after its acquisition by private equity firm Permira in January 2022. It started in my office at home in 2003 when I backed a 28-year-old who had the foresight to predict the danger of scamming and viral attacks on the internet. That success transformed my life and allowed me to be more active in investing and plenty of other things.

That aside, in 2008 I also started my own whisky company, The Last Drop Distillers Limited. Having enjoyed the pleasures of corporate life for many years, suddenly I had to travel the cheapest way possible, staying in budget hotels as I went around the world trying to see if I could build a brand on my own. After eight years the company was sold to Sazerac, a large US spirits company valued at well above $10 billion. Today, it is the pinnacle brand in their empire.

It has been an interesting journey. In 2014 I published my first book, *Making Your Marque: 100 Tips to Build Your Personal Brand and Succeed in Business*. It was republished two years ago as *Make Your Mark in the Workplace*. I believe that in the modern world, people are looking for short, pertinent, succinct bits of advice and guidance. That is why I decided to write this book: to give you guidance, including learnings from my mistakes, and to encourage you to make the right decisions on your journey through life.

In 2001 the Judging Panel of Scotch Industry Leaders awarded me "The Lifetime Achievement Award for Services to the Scotch Whisky Industry." In 2015 I was made an Honorary Fellow of the Marketing Society of Great Britain for services to marketing and brand-building globally. And, last but not least, in 2013 I was privileged to receive an OBE from Her Majesty the Queen for services to the scotch whisky industry. It is with much pride that I look back on the many brands and people I have worked with – and supported – in my 55 years in business. Today, I mentor young professionals and invest in promising start-ups. I was recently appointed chairman of The Wiltshire Whisky Distillery Company, which launched in June 2022 and will be an exciting long-term project. So, as much as I have learned in the past, I'm also proud to look to the future, too.

FOREWORD

I hope this book of succinct quotes will give you some positive and easy-to-remember tools to help you both commercially and personally throughout your career.

It is about making a success of the most important brand in your life – **"Brand You"**. It's about how you set yourself apart from others who are competing for positions or promotion and prepare yourself, hopefully as a leader of the future.

It's about viewing your personal brand as a trademark, an asset you must constantly protect while continuously moulding and shaping it. You must do this regardless of your age, your position or your profession, understanding the importance of the brand described by legendary adman Tom Peters as **"Me Inc."** If you do not brand yourself, others will, and you will have no control over the result.

So, manage your reputation, manage your image and manage the perception other people have of you. In this ever-shifting 21st century, and especially post COVID-19, your job could be gone in an instant. **Then where would your brand be?**

Your brand must be bigger than any company you work for. Wherever you go in life, your brand will go with you. This book will guide you as you **build your brand, make your way through life and play your part in making the world a better place.**

In this fast-changing world, you will thrive if you can learn how best to react to things you cannot change, from the impact of globalization to climate change. As you choose which organization to work for or start your own business, consider what it offers not just in terms of growth and profit, but in improving the world you live in.

And it is always essential to be genuine. As Oscar Wilde noted, "Be yourself – everyone else is already taken."

Why a book of quotes?

Very often witty, hopefully always wise, quotes are a powerful way to encapsulate an idea, make it land with an audience, and leave a lasting impression.

A simple quote can be the most liberating moment of the day and immediately bring balance to our mindset. Quotes are a quick, concise and timely burst of wisdom to get our focus back. They express optimism and insight, and they awaken hope, motivation, encouragement, inspiration, positivity, light and happiness.

In this era of social media, a soundbite is as good as an essay. I have used quotes to great effect throughout my career in marketing and brand-building, and I've always found them to be a highly effective communication tool. This book summarizes some of the best wisdom around in memorable quotes you can carry with you throughout the day.

Good quotes provide both moral and actionable guidance – they can change the direction of our day and even our life.

I have credited the authors of these gems wherever possible, drawn many more quotes from my own public speaking or common parlance, and seek forgiveness if anyone has gone unacknowledged.

PART 1
BRAND YOU AND ACCELERATING YOUR CAREER

CHAPTER 1
HOW TO BUILD YOUR PERSONAL BRAND

1. If you don't design your own life plan, chances are you'll fall into someone else's. And guess what they have planned for you? Not much.
Jim Rohn, American entrepreneur and author

2. If you don't know where you're going, any road will take you there.

If you don't know where you're going, any road will take you there.

At the very least, have a vision of what you wish to do or achieve for the **next three years**.

This will give you a path to follow, galvanize you with the prospect of the success to come, and you can evaluate your progress every six months to keep on track.

Include some personal wellbeing goals along with your business ambitions.

3. A goal without a plan is just a wish.

Antoine de Saint-Exupéry, author of The Little Prince

4. Doing what you like is freedom, but liking what you do is real happiness.

5. Control your own future – otherwise, circumstances beyond your control will take control of you!

Of course, we would all love to be able to control our future, and it is far easier said than done. You can help yourself by realizing that understanding your environment – both external and internal – will give you a real advantage.

External factors are **uncontrollable variables**. Clearly, these are factors over which you have no personal control, from COVID-19 to Brexit, the US presidency to the state of the economy. But that does not mean you can ignore them. Instead, you should read up on each of them so you have some understanding of the impact they can have on your situation, giving you a broader background when making decisions.

Next come **semi-controllable variables**, which can be modified (albeit with some work) to adapt to changing needs. They include the structure of an organization, its culture and leadership style. They apply to government and any company where you work.

Last come the internal factors that are **controllable variables**. Essentially these are the resources a company can leverage, such as finance, marketing, IT and people. For your personal and professional development, they include education, training and amassing extra skills. But they are also internal to you – the qualities that will help you thrive, including mental resilience, physical and emotional health.

Understanding these can help you in deciding what industry you want to work in, which companies you will target and, if you are starting your own business, the strongest opportunities ahead.

6. Life isn't about finding yourself. Life is about creating yourself.

George Bernard Shaw, playwright

Brands need to be constantly built and refreshed. They should never be taken for granted. The same principle applies to Brand You.

7. The positive thinker sees the invisible, feels the intangible and achieves the impossible.

Winston Churchill, former UK Prime Minister and war leader

8. Reject rejection – it is a fact of life you have to deal with.

When you apply for any job, especially in our digital world, you will inevitably experience a lot of rejection. Most of the time, you will not even receive a reply and when you do, more often than not, it will be a **no**. This is hardly ever personal; it is simply that far more people apply for jobs than there are jobs available.

So be persistent and keep your spirits up.

9. The only place where success comes before work is in the dictionary.

10. Efforts and courage are not enough without purpose and direction.

John F. Kennedy, former US President

11. Luck is the intersection of hard work and opportunity.

12. Success is no accident. It is hard work, perseverance, learning, studying, sacrifice and most of all... love of what you are doing or learning to do.

Pelé, Brazilian football legend

13. What doesn't kill you makes you stronger.

This popular phrase, derived from the 19th-century philosopher Nietzsche, suggests that every experience brings us some benefit.

We should never neglect, however, the toll on our mental health from disappointments and setbacks. Knowing where to find support and having the courage to ask for it are what make us stronger.

14. When you are sliding down the banisters of life, you cannot expect all the splinters to be facing in the right direction.

When you are sliding down the banisters of life, you cannot expect all the splinters to be facing in the right direction.

However...

15. If you never leave the shore, you will never reach the other side.

16. It takes many years and hard work to become an overnight success.

17. The world is not shaped by opinions – it is shaped by what one is prepared to do.

Leaders good and bad make things happen, whether they are in government, such as Vladimir Putin and Xi Jinping, Boris Johnson and Joe Biden, or in business.

In business, the top leaders are visionaries who spotted the gap and went for it, creating companies such as Amazon, Google, Tesla, Facebook and more.

Establish your own brand by making your mark as you make your way through life.

18. As you build Brand You, it's not enough to be known for what you do – you must be known for what you do differently.

A prime example is Elon Musk, the founder of Tesla and SpaceX. His ventures have ripped up the rule book and got the whole world talking.

19. An investment in knowledge pays the best interest.

Benjamin Franklin, Founding Father of the United States

20. If it is to be, it's up to me.

Ben Hogan, American golfer

21. We are what we repeatedly do. Excellence, therefore, is not an act but a habit.

Aristotle, ancient Greek philosopher

This reminds me to put in the effort on the days I am not feeling motivated. Success comes from consistent good work, not a good day here and there.

22. Your reputation is what people say about you when you leave the room.

Jeff Bezos, founder of Amazon

Lack of ego, less use of the word "I" and being interested in other people are all part of what shapes the impression they have of you.

23. You gain more by making others look good than by singing your own praises.

24. One of the things that we learned early on was that you don't have all the answers, and when you think you do, you're wrong.
Ian Kantor, founder of Investec

No one is an expert, and I often light-heartedly say an "ex" is a has-been while a "spurt" is a drip under pressure.

The trick is to be calmly confident in a positive way, without acting as if you know everything. Because no one does.

25. When you are invited to interview, your first test is the way you treat the receptionist.

26. The truth sometimes hurts. Facing personal truths may be painful, but equally it can help you face the future positively.

Every five years, carry out a personal audit of your strengths and weaknesses. In doing so, seek truthful views from people you trust and make sure they offer their genuine opinion rather than sycophantic praise.

And if the truth feels painful, do not be shy in seeking support when it comes to addressing the room for improvement that your audit has exposed.

---

27. Don't believe in your own hype.

As you climb the corporate ladder, remember never to confuse the person you are with the position you hold. The privileges, perks and invitations you receive are not for you, they are just for the temporary tenant of that job title.

So don't let things go to your head: a title is a means to an end, not an end in itself.

CHAPTER 2
GREAT COMMUNICATION

Great communication is a necessity, and a skill
worth rehearsing.

28. Make AIDA your theme song! Attention – Interest – Desire – Action

First impressions count… and you only have two minutes to make a positive connection! I recommend you embrace a technique I call AIDA: Attention – Interest – Desire – Action.

Most people have a very short attention span and are only interested in you because of what you can do for them. Apply AIDA and you'll make more of a splash socially, in your romantic life and in every aspect of business – be it selling yourself or your product, meeting and influencing people, or working out what someone is hoping to get from you!

- **ATTENTION**: Look people firmly in the eyes and do not hesitate to ask questions.
- **INTEREST**: Ask questions to get their interest, which will allow you in turn to address your agenda.
- **DESIRE**: Be succinct and focused for maximum effect… and all being well, what follows is a positive result for you –
- **ACTION**!

29. A picture says a thousand words.

A picture says a thousand words.

When making a speech, good slides or pictures can be very powerful. They also allow you time to pause while the audience absorbs the image.

30. A smart person knows what to say. A wise person knows whether to say it or not.

31. You learned your best social skills face to face – now apply them to those Zoom and Skype meetings.

Great eye contact and honing your message are the keys here. Remember to look into your camera, not the person on the screen, and have a crib sheet out of sight so you can make all your comments succinctly.

32. You have two ears and one mouth, so use them proportionately.

Most people are talkers rather than listeners – I'm an inveterate talker myself. It is amazing what a good impression you make when you ask someone to tell you about themselves and engage them in a genuine conversation.

In other words, it is a dialogue, not a monologue!

33. Courage is what it takes to stand up and speak; courage is also what it takes to sit down and listen.
Winston Churchill

34. Before you speak, THINK.

- T – Is it true?
- H – Is it helpful?
- I – Is it inspiring?
- N – Is it necessary?
- K – Is it kind?

35. If you cannot explain it simply, you don't understand it well enough.
Albert Einstein, Nobel Prize-winning physicist
And...

36. If you want to understand something, teach it to someone else.

37. Less said effectively is far better than more said hurriedly.
Useful advice if you are making a presentation or a speech: do not rush to cram in more than you really have time for, or you risk confusing and overloading your audience.

38. It is good to have a large vocabulary, but even better to use it sparingly.
No one appreciates a show-off... and you will sometimes make a better impression by *listening.*

39. Learn to listen. Opportunity sometimes knocks very softly.

40. Present yourself as you wish to be perceived.

"So, why haven't I got the job?"

When applying for a job and whenever you are at work, always dress professionally. Do your research and choose clothes that fit the setting, whether that is a suit for a corporate meeting or an eye-catching T-shirt for a social event.

I once got a job for one key reason… my brightly shining shoes. My rival and I were equally qualified, but only I had shoes that were spotlessly polished. I later found out the CEO regarded this as a vital sign of serious intent. His principle was simple: "If you can't take care of your shoes, how will you take care of my business?"

41. Don't Zoom away your credibility.
Cindy Ann Peterson, My Style, My Way

Your attire and grooming are some of the simplest things you can do to maintain your professional bearing, as Cindy points out.

You may be on a Zoom call from your home office (aka your bedroom), but team those pyjama bottoms with an appropriate top… and never stand up while the camera is still on!

Ensuring your backdrop looks equally tidy means the only judgement people make about your appearance will be a positive one.

42. The most important thing in communication is hearing what isn't said.

Professor Peter Drucker, author and management consultant

Look to body language for clues as to what people really mean.

---

43. Your body language and voice should match what you are saying.

Body language is a key component to job seeking or engaging with a prospective client.

Make others feel important by paying close attention to them. The eyes are the windows of the soul, so ensure you make eye contact. Looking away will not give them confidence in you.

Listen carefully and pause before replying, rather than jumping in.

Hands are our most important tool: show your hands so you don't look shifty and use them (in moderation) to give your story emphasis.

Interviewers or potential clients will start making judgements about you within milliseconds: from the way you sit in reception to how you greet them. They will then spend the rest of the interview or meeting simply gathering data to confirm that initial impression. It's known as confirmation bias. If you take too long to warm up, it's too late.

---

44. Trust me.

It's always alarming to hear this. Surely, we should be able to trust our colleagues all the time, so this immediately makes me suspicious.

45. I want to be honest with you.

I dread this phrase! My reply is always, "Aren't you normally?"

46. There are a number of universal social criteria – place, language, food, worldview, interests, sense of humour and institutions. Use them!

Across the globe people use the same criteria to decide who they want as a friend or a team member. If you want to influence someone, do some research to tick as many of these boxes as possible.

47. CV stands for Complete Veracity, not Can't Vouch for this...

When constructing a CV, never exaggerate your credentials. The truth will always emerge – often online – and you will be the loser.

When applying for a job and attaching your truthful CV, make it clear from the start how you can help the company you are applying to.

CHAPTER 3
LEARNING FROM MISTAKES

48. The only people who never fail are those who never try!

You will also have heard the phrase, "Nothing ventured, nothing gained." It is about taking calculated risks and being bold. It is why one of the criteria for winning Ernst & Young's prestigious Entrepreneur of the Year Award is to be "an independent thinker who is willing to take risks in the face of uncertainty."

We will all get things wrong from time to time. What is important is to learn from each experience and keep looking forward.

49. If you fail, never give up. F.A.I.L. means "First Attempt In Learning".

And if you get NO for an answer, remember N.O. means "Next Opportunity".

50. Learn from experience of the past – then look forward and focus on the future.

And…

51. You drive a car by looking through the windscreen, not the rear-view mirror.

52. Experience is only valuable if you adapt it to the current market.

Joseph Petyan, advertising executive

53. Most good judgement comes from experience. And experience comes from making many mistakes.

Most good judgement comes from experience. And experience comes from making many mistakes.

54. It is fine to celebrate success, but it is more important to heed the lessons of failure.

Bill Gates, founder of Microsoft

Failure is not to have an idea which doesn't succeed; failure is not to have an idea.

55. Learn from the mistakes of others; you can't live long enough to make them all yourself.

Eleanor Roosevelt, former First Lady of the United States

56. It is impossible to live without failing at something, unless you live so cautiously that you might as well not have lived at all, in which case you have failed by default.

J.K. Rowling, author of the Harry Potter *series*

57. Winners are most often people who have made mistakes, but do not quit.

58. The key to success is to acknowledge mistakes whilst learning from them – and tenaciously applying this enhanced wisdom to future opportunities.
Life can often seem or be very tough, but it will help in difficult times to be thankful for all the good things you have. You don't have to be better than everybody else, you just have to be better than you were a week ago. Progress comes from incremental steps.

59. Success is not final; failure is not fatal. It is the courage to continue that counts.

Winston Churchill

60. One of the great things about experience – very much including mistakes – is that you can pass it on to the next generation.

61. Happiness is like a butterfly.

Happiness is like a butterfly:
the more you chase it, the more it will elude you.
But if you turn your attention to other things,
it comes and softly sits on your shoulder.

62. Only those who dare to fail greatly can ever achieve greatly.
Robert F. Kennedy, former United States Attorney General

CHAPTER 4
HOW TO ACCELERATE YOUR CAREER

Use the first 20 years of your career to learn and grow, shaping the direction of Brand You. The next 20 years will determine how well you do commercially and how you capitalize financially on your brand. Finally, as you move toward retirement, you can reinvent yourself as a niche brand or elder statesperson.

63. Clever thinking – 8 Cs for building your career

1. Culture – stems from leadership, not what people say, but what they do
2. Competence – built from experience
3. Customer focus – leads to customer loyalty
4. Curiosity – not complacency
5. Composure – be calm like a swan, but paddle furiously beneath if necessary
6. Collaboration – very much about attitude and hiring the right people
7. Courage – to do the right thing, have honest conversations and create a considerate culture
8. Confidence – to back your judgement... but after listening to others

64. Fail to prepare, prepare to fail.
Adapted from Benjamin Franklin

This goes whether you are applying for a job, trying to impress your boss, or simply preparing for a meeting. Winging it is a terrible long-term strategy!

65. Education is your personal escalator.

Completing a degree or a practical qualification is never a burden – see it instead as an escalator for your career.

In fact, you may need to constantly retrain to adapt and prosper in the future. In our rapidly changing world, you can never assume that what you do now is how it should be done tomorrow.

66. Willing horses get overloaded.

Willing horses get overloaded.

It is good to go the extra mile, but beware of taking on so much that you become a busy fool and achieve little of substance. It is often said that 10 per cent of the people do 90 per cent of the real work.

If your managers offload lots of projects onto you, you may find you do five jobs moderately well rather than two or three extremely well. You will not receive the recognition you deserve and could even be criticized for the quality of your work.

67. More people work at keeping their job than doing it well.

If you are the former, you are leading a meaningless life. If you are the latter, keep up the good work!

68. In tough times, never be afraid to ask for help.

Often the person you ask will feel good as a result, so you will have made two people happier!

And do not hesitate to ask senior people questions – it shows commitment and interest.

If you have a serious problem, you should be able to share it with a decent boss. But also take along your best suggestion for solving it, so that they can debate, add to, or amend your ideas and then share responsibility with you, whatever happens.

69. Whatever you think privately, give the new boss a positive welcome.

This is all about giving yourself enough time to form a proper judgement after observing how they interact with the team and guide you all.

70. Smile more!

This has been my mantra since long before the phrase "talk less, smile more" found fame in the musical *Hamilton*.

Making an active decision to smile more is good for you and those you meet. If you have a family, you can learn a great deal from your children, especially about patience and tolerance. Do you know it takes the average 40-something ten weeks to laugh as much as a four-year-old does in one day? Start putting that right!

71. As you climb the ladder, make conversations about "them" not "you".

This technique is a great door opener and helps build relationships. Asking people about themselves and their projects, rather than talking about yourself, is not just polite… it is productive.

72. It is amazing how much we get done around here when nobody cares who gets the credit.

Keith M. Kent, American educator

73. When someone else's candle is lit, it doesn't cause yours to go out. It just adds more light to the room. So, when you allow someone to shine, it doesn't diminish you – it makes the whole room brighter.

74. You don't need to see the top of the staircase to take the first few steps – you just need the courage to begin climbing.

75. Ideally you should seek to have a personal appraisal twice a year.

A good company will have it built into the system. It is a great opportunity to stress your loyalty to the company (no matter what you really think) and to seek guidance from your manager as to how you can advance your career.

76. Be nice to people on the way up and, with luck, they may remember you on the way down.

Be nice to people on the way up and, with luck, they may remember you on the way down.

77. There is no "I" in team.

People work with you, not for you. I love the acronym TEAM: Together Everyone Achieves More.

78. Even if you think "I", always say "we".

Yes, maybe it was your idea, or you led the project… but could you really have made it work without anybody else?

Share praise, be inclusive, learn to step back from the spotlight and recognize the important part every individual contributes to collective success. You will be rewarded many times over.

79. Take care of your thoughts when you are alone and take care of your words when you are with people.

This is about looking after your own emotional wellbeing and respecting the feelings of others. We are generally stronger together and forging both personal friendships and business relationships is mutually beneficial. When they combine, so much the better.

80. Be wary of spending time with people who talk badly of others. Know that as soon as you leave the group, you will be the next topic.

81. Imagination is crucial for finding and creating new opportunities, especially in a crisis.

82. Successful people read daily, compliment others, embrace change, forgive, seek new ideas, continually learn, have a sense of gratitude, set goals and have life plans.

Unsuccessful people criticize often, fear change and hold grudges, yet think they know it all and blame others for their failures.

Look around and follow the example of people worthy of respect.

CHAPTER 5
CHANGING JOBS

83. Choose a job you like, and you will never have to work a day in your life.

Confucius, ancient Chinese philosopher

84. If you would hit the mark, you must aim high. For every arrow that flies feels the attraction of Earth.

Henry Wadsworth Longfellow, American poet

If you would hit the mark, you must aim high. For every arrow
that flies feels the attraction of Earth.

85. Be loyal but don't expect loyalty in return.

There may come a day when you are fired. When a business decides to make people redundant, I'm afraid loyalty often counts for nothing.

Sometimes losing your job may be the price of doing what you believe is right. I was sacked over 20 years ago for launching a new whisky, Chivas Regal 18. It is now the world leader in that age category. I did it against the wishes of the company chairman... whose father had invented its predecessor, Chivas Regal 12!

86. It is often said that your network is your net worth.

At times you may not feel like going out to an event or getting together online, but don't reject opportunities to meet people. A stranger is just a friend you don't yet know.

In our fast, pressurized world, it is also good for your mental wellbeing and the wellbeing of those around you.

87. Nurture your network.

Networking is a crucial part of business. Join associations, attend events, accept invitations.

Always be ready to exchange details, take the time to remember people's names and use them when you are next in conversation. Giving is an important element of branding, and the most successful networkers give value before expecting to receive it.

It is often said the best way to be successful is to make others successful first.

Build a good digital database of those you meet – you never know when you might need it.

88. Always be a good leaver, whatever you think.

So, you have secured your dream new job, and you are done with the rabble you are leaving behind – not so fast. Bad-mouth your old firm, and word will reach your new employers that you are mean-spirited and disloyal... and if your old boss one day turns up again as your new boss, you will have a big hole to dig yourself out of.

What's more, you never know when you might want to come back. The struggling company you are leaving could become a world beater in a few years.

89. Good fortune often happens when opportunity meets with preparation.

Thomas Edison, inventor

In other words, you can make your own luck!

Rather than waiting for that golden chance to drop into your lap, go out and make it happen.

90. Look where a company is going. Not just where it has been.

When you are looking for a new job, it is tempting to target companies with a famous name and long track record. But it is more useful to look at where a company is going.

Being a big brand with an impressive heritage is no protection against going bust, as many one-time giants of the High Street have recently proved. Younger businesses, on the other hand, can be more dynamic and constantly evolve to keep loyal customers excited.

91. Look before you leap to a new job – the grass often looks greener on the other side of the fence.

The grass often looks greener on the other side of the fence.

Today people change jobs at the drop of a hat. Remember, the grass is greener on the other side of the fence because there is often more manure on the other side.

You never know the strength and value of Brand You until you leave your present situation – be it a country, a job or to start your own business. Then you will also find out what people really think of you.

If you are headhunted for a new job, do not resign from your company without a firm written contract. And if you are in demand, obtain an exit contract at the start of your new post. You may need it one day, as I found out many years ago. I was very keen to work for the firm but had noticed that people did not seem to stay there very long. So right from the word go, I asked for a two-year rolling notice exit deal. When I later fell out with the chairman and had to leave, knowing I would be paid for another two years gave me invaluable breathing space.

92. A business relationship without a future is like sitting in a car without wheels. You can stay in it all you want, but it isn't going anywhere.

93. Great companies train people well enough so that they can leave – but equally, treat them well enough so they don't want to.

Make this your mantra when you become CEO.

94. Do not be ashamed of losing your job.

It happens at some stage to most people. Accept it, deal with it, learn from it and move on.

PART 2
**BUILDING AND BOOSTING
COMPANY BRANDS**

CHAPTER 6
KNOW YOUR CUSTOMER

95. There is only one boss: the customer. And he can fire everybody in the company from the chairman down, simply by spending his money somewhere else.
Sam Walton, founder of Walmart

As you progress through corporate life and report to different people, never forget that without the client, customer or consumer, there is no business.

The customer pays your mortgage, buys your car, funds your trips to restaurants and the theatre and pays for your holidays. Treat them appropriately!

---

96. The only truly good customer is a repeat customer.

Spend as much time as you can talking to real customers. Too many companies are bureaucratic machines that have forgotten why they are in business.

A repeat sale shows you are building your brand and have a relationship with your customers.

Customer complaints should be seen positively as a way to encourage continual improvement and generate more business.

---

97. Price is what you pay. Value is what you get.
Benjamin Graham, British-born American economist

Good marketing is essentially about profitability, but many businesses struggle to pitch their products at the right price. The secret is providing consumers with products and services they need at a price that makes both the customer and the company happy.

A great example comes from The Championships, Wimbledon, just around the corner from my home. Strawberries and cream are inseparable from the Wimbledon brand, and you might think there would be room to exploit tennis lovers willing to pay for the full experience. Far from it – the punnets are actually very reasonably priced.

Result: customers are delighted, and Wimbledon effortlessly burnishes its feelgood image.

98. It is not important to win awards; it is essential to win and retain customers.

99. If the shoe fits...

You must always put yourself in your customer's shoes. If you do not look after them, your competitors will. Make sure all your marketing gives people an unbeatable reason to choose your business and/or brand.

100. You have more customers than you know.

Building relationships with everyone in the supply chain en route to the consumer is a critical plank in building a sound business. Your product may go through importers and wholesalers before reaching its end user, so treat them as customers too, considerately and carefully. Without them, you have no consumers.

101. If you are successful, you do not have customers – you have loyal friends.

102. Fight for what you believe.

Great brands are almost invariably created by entrepreneurs or individuals in companies who have the vision and courage to fight for what they believe.

Coca-Cola was originally sold in pharmacies as a medicine, then customers started reporting that not only was it a great hangover cure, but they loved the taste… and suddenly it had massive potential. The company had to tear up its marketing plan, rethink its branding and believe in its ability to turn an unpromising-looking product into a best seller.

103. Products are made, but customers buy brands.

Perception is reality.

Never forget:

Products are about **INTRINSIC** physical attributes. What is the product and what does it do?

Brands are about the **EXTRINSIC** packaging, as well as the wants, needs and values that link to your consumer's aspirations.

Vodka is the perfect example. It is supposed to be odourless, colourless and tasteless. Usually made from grain, molasses, grape or potato spirit, it is heavily filtered and cleaned. It is very difficult to tell the difference between one vodka and another and, if you add ice and cola, almost impossible.

So why would you pay £20 for Absolut or £50 for a niche vodka rather than £10 for a cheap bottle? The answer is that perception is reality. Marketers have spent millions creating a brand image, and customers buy into those extrinsic feelgood factors.

104. Marketing is not a battle of products; it is a battle of perceptions.

Al Ries and Jack Trout, authors of The 22 Immutable Laws of Marketing

Customers purchase with their eyes and their imagination. When you cook a steak, the sizzle sets the scene, coupled with the delightful aroma. It is then the inherent product, the steak, which completes the picture.

When you buy a canned product you cannot see, the brand name becomes more important.

105. There are products which people need, and products which people want. That is why there is a luxury goods market.

Karl Lagerfeld, former creative director of Chanel and king of haute couture

106. Fashions come and go but style endures.

Coco Chanel, founder of Chanel and fashion icon

The perfume Chanel No. 5, one of the great brands of all time, celebrated its centenary in 2021 with the same wonderful scent, consistent packaging and masterful messaging that it has always deployed.

107. If you want to charge a premium for a service or product, make sure no one else can offer what you do – at least for a while.

Here are my rules for premium branding:

- Be confident and self-focused
- Tell a good story
- Leave room for the consumer to imagine...

108. Research is an aid to judgement, not a substitute.

It is rather like a drunk leaning against a lamppost. Is it for support or illumination or both?

It will not tell you how to get home but may offer some clues to get you started!

109. Never forget that numbers, which are often the substance of market research, can be impostors.

There is a feeling that facts and figures carry all truth and are the primary keys to decision making. In fact, your opinion and judgement often have a higher value.

110. Constant vigilance!

When building brands and companies, very much including Brand You, success is determined by doing well consistently – not just from time to time. Constant vigilance is required (to quote Mad-Eye Moody in the *Harry Potter* series).

111. Welcome professional competitors; the worst problem for a business is complacency and smugness.

Remember the Inverse Law of Success – success often leads to arrogance and arrogance to failure.

CHAPTER 7
PEOPLE: YOUR MOST IMPORTANT ASSET

112. Your greatest asset is your people.

The key to a great business is, therefore, to pick and motivate staff. You may have a brilliant business proposition but without good, enthusiastic employees, it will fail.

Give them plenty of space to operate, back the team, keep asking questions and act on their answers.

More than ever your employees are your real brand ambassadors. Top management needs to be very aware of staff insights, feedback and complaints.

113. Mankind is a social animal and companies are social organizations, at their best when men and women enjoy productive, successful lives.

114. Successful managers hire people with personality and character – not just qualifications.

Qualifications, no matter how many, are purely a means to an end – not an end in themselves. It is personality that galvanizes others, brings a dream alive and forges the most productive business relationships. It is character that staff will respect, admire and replicate.

115. People are central to the success of any business, so a wise businessperson does their best to understand the team and the people who build it.

116. Beware of parachute management.

Beware of parachute management.

Brands are built by people with passion and commitment over time, so too many staff changes risks killing delicate young brands.

117. Relationship capital is priceless and needs constant investment.

In a digital age, it is more necessary than ever.

118. If you want to go fast, go alone. If you want to go further, go together.

119. Empower people by encouraging them – that's how brands are made.

In the early 1980s when I took over as the head of the International Distillers & Vintners (IDV) UK operation, I asked for and took the advice of 67 managers, then used their ideas to improve the business. This gave the staff a greater sense of belonging to the company, and I treated them with compassion and respect. Seeking the views of those managers was just the first step.

The result: profits that had been flat for some time soared threefold in four years – thanks to the team effort.

120. It is people who make it happen.

Throughout my career I have wanted people to know they were working *with* me, not *for* me. However apparently humble their role, I wanted them to feel important. The cleaner is not the person with the mop and bucket… they are the person responsible for showcasing your HQ to the world at its very best.

121. Your people are not commodities to be treated badly and often as disposable – they are priceless assets.

I hate seeing rude, arrogant senior executives with no time or respect for those lower down the food chain.

122. Helping one person may not change the world – but it may change one person's world.

123. Look for talent in unusual places.

Look for talent in unusual places.

In one of my first management jobs in the alcohol industry, I hired a teetotaller – very rare in the drinks business at that time.

124. Avoid surprises: if there is a problem, tell your people immediately so it can be resolved quickly.

125. A sense of humour is part of the act of leadership, of getting along with people, of getting things done.

Dwight D. Eisenhower, former US President and General

CHAPTER 8
INNOVATION

126. Innovate or die.

Innovate or die.

127. Every company needs to make itself obsolete.

Innovation is the key to future success. Unless you can innovate and replace your core business, you will die along with it.

A good marketer has patience in building a brand but equally respects the fact that you must constantly create something better before your competitors do.

The success of Tesla says it all.

General Motors and Ford had the technology for electric cars years ago but never embraced it properly, and today Tesla is worth considerably more than both of them combined.

128. If you always do what you've always done, you'll always get what you've always got.

129. Successful corporate innovation requires a senior executive to take on the role of protector.

He or she must see that new ideas are not condemned to death before receiving a fair hearing. This is especially the case when companies purely focus on short-term profit (especially quarterly earnings).

If you wish to be an intrapreneur or innovator in a large corporation, ensure your boss supports you 100 per cent. I have both benefitted and suffered from support and the lack thereof.

130. If innovation goes wrong, don't be embarrassed about reverting to a proven idea.

Think of Coca-Cola, which now markets its "original taste since 1886"… and learned a sharp lesson when it changed the recipe in 1985. Just shy of its 100th anniversary, the company announced it would discontinue its beloved Coca-Cola in favour of a new product that millions derisively called New Coke.

New Coke was a disaster from the start, and the experiment did not last very long.

131. When you are the innovator, imitations are proof that you are heading for success.

Baileys Irish Cream failed in research, but my colleague Tom Jago believed in the brand, and it was launched in 1974. Today it is the number-one liqueur in the world, with many imitators.

132. Most new brands fail, but one terrific success will make up for a string of failures.

You must take risks if you are going to get anywhere.

133. The future belongs to those who see the possibilities before they are obvious, then galvanize resources and energies effectively to attain them.

---

134. Innovation requires passion

New brands and products will be the result of painstaking market analysis as much as emotion, but you need passion when you're masterminding a new launch. You will have to love the process and support your team to overcome the difficulties you are certain to experience en route to victory.

---

135. Great companies encourage "intrapreneurial" thinking.

They have staff who think like entrepreneurs: challenging ingrained ideas, being creative and persistent, just like Tom Jago, inventor of Baileys Irish Cream. When it failed in research, Tom believed in it so much that he hid the results. It now has annual sales of some 7 million cases. He was right!

136. Change leader, change thyself.

To thrive in an age of disruption, leaders must build two sustainable and integrated engines: one that generates innovation and the other that delivers business transformation.

Change is an everyday part of business life, and leaders constantly need to adapt to thrive. They also need to be able to instil a culture of change amongst staff at all levels.

McKinsey Research has taken this a stage further, urging, "Change leader, change thyself." I couldn't agree more. If those who are leading change adopt a change mindset and *learn how to learn*, they can inspire their colleagues and staff with confidence.

Just one word of caution: if you are brought in as a change agent, make sure you have a champion on the board to support you.

137. A camel is a racehorse designed by a committee.

Among the greatest barriers to innovation are committees – which is why I prefer advisory boards. In my view committees create nothing. They are too often a talking shop where all the members argue, then vote on a decision that may not represent the best ideas in the room.

With advisory boards, on the other hand, everyone has the chance to express a strong opinion, but the chair decides. The members then have a duty of loyalty to support the decision made.

138. No, no, no! Beware of Dr. Nos and corporate bureaucracy.

I am not channelling Margaret Thatcher's infamous 1990 message to Europe here. Rather, I am reflecting on the fact that when it comes to change, many companies sadly have lots of Dr. Nos who avoid making decisions but are quick to criticize new initiatives from others.

Decision-making by committee and corporate bureaucracy just fuel this problem.

I have never seen a statue dedicated to a committee.

139. I believe the best committees are made up of an odd number – and three is too many.

Lew Grade, British entertainment mogul
Humorous, but you do need a genuine decision-maker.

140. Don't let red tape strangle great ideas.

The larger the corporation, the more bureaucratic and political it becomes – another barrier to innovation. While 80 per cent of your focus should be on the consumer, who is the ultimate boss, and only 20 per cent on process, the converse often unfortunately applies in big business.

It is therefore essential to streamline internal communication to sell ideas and innovation through the system and avoid relying on opaque and divisive committees.

141. It was once said that a consultant borrows your watch and charges you for the time. Now it is said that a consultant is someone with an ego so big they cannot work for a single company.

Too many people do not have the courage to tap the talent inside the corporation and thus, often as a cop-out, call in expensive consultants to lead change and innovation. Of course, they can add great value – but only if correctly deployed and directed.

142. A consultant is someone who saves his client almost enough to pay his fee.

Arnold H. Glasgow, American humourist
Before bringing in outside consultants, remember that too many people dispensing advice are full-time consultants who have no personal experience, as they have never done it themselves.

Professional advisors, such as accountants and lawyers, are essential in the highly regulated corporate world, but their advice should be kept in proportion.

CHAPTER 9
TAMING TECHNOLOGY

143. Protect your business by having a cybersecurity mindset at all times.

It is crucial for every business to take cybersecurity seriously. From loss of revenue, reputation damage and lost productivity, the consequences of being hit by hackers or a takedown can be severe.

Always keep software up to date and install robust antivirus protection. Use strong passwords and encryption, be vigilant with email and internet use, and be careful what you share online. Finally, ensure data is backed up.

According to research from the Ponemon Institute, the average cost of a data breach is $3.86 million!

144. Never send an email or post something online in anger.

You can never retract it, and it could seriously damage your career. Be wary of responding to issues when you are feeling angry – take a break or sleep on it.

Never send an email you would not like your boss to see. Who knows who has access to that email account?

And never put anything in an email that you would not want to see on the front page of a national newspaper.

145. The globe is being homogenized by the Republic of Technologies.

I wrote this in an article published 30 years ago. It is even truer today, with data being manipulated by crooks and governments all over the world!

146. In today's world there is no place to hide.

In today's world there is no place to hide.

147. Carefully look after the physical security of all devices.

Having physical access to a device makes it child's play for an attacker to extract or corrupt information. So be very careful, particularly in public or easily accessible areas.

148. Beware of paralysis by analysis.

We are drowning in data. There has been more created in the last two years than in the history of humankind. But do not forget the importance of gut feeling and instinct. Data is to help you make decisions, not avoid them.

149. Social media can be like a sewer... what you put in, you get out.

150. Don't be tempted to rest on your laurels.

Technology is constantly evolving, and companies need to move with it. With any transformation programme, it is vital to involve frontline teams and customers in the design of solutions. These are the people who understand the true challenges that need to be addressed, and they will be your biggest detractors when the change does not solve these challenges.

151. You have two feet – use them.

Email, WhatsApp and instant messages are not the best medium for diplomacy. Do not spend time bombarding people inside the company with emails – go and talk to them instead, safe working practices permitting.

152. A handshake is worth 1,000 emails.

Post-COVID crisis, nothing beats face-to-face dialogue.

153. Artificial intelligence (AI) is here to stay – understand it and use it both in business and at home to help you stay ahead.

154. Ditch Zoom and get in the room!

Luke Johnson, The Sunday Times, *20 December 2020*

Notwithstanding the wonders of technology and remote working, no amount of Zoom calls can replace creativity and teamwork from genuine face-to-face meetings.

CHAPTER 10
DOING BUSINESS INTERNATIONALLY

155. Never let language or culture prevent you from listening to what someone has to say.

You may be out of your comfort zone and English may not be your client or supplier's first language. But a good international businessperson spends time visiting the marketplace, smiling, listening and enjoying the local cuisine.

If you turn down the food, avoid mixing with the people, or ignore their customs and traditions, you might as well stay at home.

Respect difference, recognize the advantage of fusion… and charm your hosts!

156. Respect and learn from every culture and never assume yours is better.

157. Getting to know you, getting to know all about you.

To quote the song from the musical *The King and I*, I have found that the preference in Asia for taking time to get to know a colleague, supplier or business partner is much more conducive to long-term business relationships than the Western tendency to jump to instant judgement.

As the character Anna sings in the next line, "Getting to like you, getting to hope you like me."

158. Yes.

When conducting international business in a foreign language, be careful of the word "yes." In some cultures, it does not mean, "I agree with you," but simply, "I hear what you are saying."

I learned this important message in the 1970s when I started doing business in Japan.

159. Never come back from a working trip abroad with a suntan.

Never come back from a working trip abroad with a suntan.

160. Better safe than sorry... so always respect local rules and culture.

Wherever you go, be cautious, especially if you do not know the country. You can check the latest information on your destination on the Foreign, Commonwealth and Development Office website.

If you are on your own, make sure you have copies of your passport and useful documents, and back up key phone numbers. Check that your company has comprehensively insured you for your trip, and that it understands its duty of care. And beware of alcohol on a plane – altitude makes you drunk much faster.

Business travel can be very demanding, so be sure to allow yourself enough time to prepare for a meeting, get to the venue and recover afterwards.

---

161. Consumer needs transcend geographic boundaries and cultures.

This is what underlies hopes for global brand-building. With a streamlined website and fast delivery, you should be able to rapidly boost your global sales.

But there are pitfalls along the way...

---

162. Following global diktats rather than strategic guidance is a recipe for local failure.

The masterplan dreamed up at HQ may not work on the ground. You will need to be agile, responsive to local conditions and ready to learn from those you've come to sell to.

163. You can't succeed without motivated distributors and passionate local brand champions.

Think hard about how you will motivate, enthuse and reward them... before your competitors come up with a better offer.

164. Never forget that a global brand is nothing more than a local brand replicated many, many times.

165. Look East but take care.

By 2025 China will overtake the USA as the world's leading economic powerhouse, so this is a market worth investigating carefully.

Make sure you have sound advice on operating legally and conforming to local protocol. On the other hand, you should also act early and firmly to protect your brand for the long term.

Intellectual property violations are endemic in China, so plan your branding, then register and monitor your brand with pinpoint attention. And do not forget that patience is a virtue.

Also remember that Asia is not one country: it is the largest multi-cultural melting pot on the planet.

166. Ask the lawyers.

Wherever you are trading, from India to Indianapolis, make sure you carefully understand the law and all legal documents you are shown.

I was once badly burned by lending money to someone I thought was a friend without adequate legal paperwork.

167. Before rushing to do business abroad, think carefully about "home sweet home".

COVID-19 and the war in Ukraine have revealed the fragility of international relations, the risks of international interdependence and the vulnerability of global supply chains.

These shattering experiences are adding pressure on governments and businesses to rethink their global dependencies. If you can, there is value in looking in your own backyard first. Trading there might not be so lucrative... but more reliable and secure.

PART 3
PERSONAL VALUES

CHAPTER 11
TIME MANAGEMENT

168. Someday is not a day of the week.

Establish a plan for what you wish to achieve at the start of the week, then spend a few minutes reviewing what you've accomplished when you have a quiet moment at the end.

169. If you do not manage your time, time will manage you.

Ten ways to make the most of your working day:

1. At the end of each day, plan your priorities for the next day in order of importance.
2. The Pareto principle states that 80 per cent of your success comes from 20 per cent of your activity. Determine what is important and plan your day accordingly.
3. Yes, we have busy diaries, but factor in time for interruptions such as phone calls and urgent emails – you must have breathing space.
4. You cannot answer every call or respond to every email instantly. Switch electronics off if you need to. An immediate response to everything out of habit is not always good business.
5. Set yourself deadlines to complete tasks and schedule these in your calendar.
6. Before any meeting or call, reflect on what you want to get out of it. Afterwards, work out what you have achieved. It will make you more efficient.

7. It is important to learn to delegate, especially if you are an entrepreneur, for whom it is often a struggle. Learn to hand out less important tasks or outsource.
8. If you have many calls to make, hang a "Do Not Disturb" sign on your door or desk and work through them sequentially.
9. Be ruthless with meetings. Always set an agenda and a finishing time. The average office worker spends around 16 hours in meetings each week, much of which is time wasted.
10. Get rid of distractions when you need to focus. If necessary, find a quieter bolthole.

170. Time is the scarcest resource and unless it can be managed, nothing else can be managed.

Professor Peter Drucker

171. If you're not early, you're late!

If you're not early, you're late!

Punctuality is not just a virtue, but a necessity.

Being late creates a bad impression and it can be seen as rude, so always call and apologize even if you are only running 15 minutes behind schedule.

My tip is to aim to arrive 15 minutes early every time.

172. I have always been a quarter of an hour before my time, and it had made a man of me.

Admiral Lord Nelson, victor of the Battle of Trafalgar

173. When the sun comes up, you had better be running.

Charlotte Wresting

Every morning in Africa, a gazelle wakes up. It knows it must run faster than the fastest lion or it will be killed. Every morning a lion wakes up. It knows it must outrun the slowest gazelle or it will starve to death. It doesn't matter whether you are a lion or a gazelle – when the sun comes up, you had better be running.

174. Procrastination is the thief of time.

175. Never leave till tomorrow that which you can do today.

Benjamin Franklin

176. We all have 24 hours a day. It is what we do with them that sets us apart.

Good time management is essential. It is easy to be so busy that you forget what you are trying to achieve.

177. To improve productivity, manage attention and not time.

A few hours of concentration and clear thinking, devoid of distraction, can be twice as productive as a day where you try to do too much.

178. You may wish to please everybody, but you must also learn to say no!

Sometimes it is the only way to stick to the priorities you know are important. There is a danger in not performing well because you have taken on too many tasks.

179. Beware of meetings for meetings' sake. They should always have a real purpose.

Who wishes they could attend more meetings? Too often you come out knowing there was no value in being there… or that it could have been so much more productive if only it had been better run.

Typically, we waste about 200 hours a year in unproductive meetings, according to a report in *Management Today*.

180. When the outcome of a meeting is to have another meeting, it has been a lousy meeting.
Herbert Hoover, former US President

181. There is no point wasting time worrying about things over which you have no control.

182. The smallest deed is better than the greatest intention.
John Burroughs, conservationist

183. If you spend your time in the middle of the road, you are liable to be hit from both sides.

Do not sit on the fence.

I cannot abide indecision.

184. Life's tragedy is we get old too soon and wise too late.

Benjamin Franklin

So, get on and make things happen!

185. If you want something done urgently, ask a busy person.

186. What ARE you? Your body? Your soul? Your name? None of the three. Your actions!

187. Action may not bring happiness, but there is no happiness without action.

William James, American philosopher

CHAPTER 12
HEALTH, MENTAL HEALTH AND WELLBEING

188. It is said you only live once. Wrong! We only die once, but we live every day.

189. It should be the responsibility of every manager to look after the mental health and wellbeing of the most important assets in the company – the staff.

We live in a busy world. More information means more choice, more choice means more options, more options mean more decisions. When faced with too much choice, too many options for a career, too much workload or whatever it may be, we can freeze.

I believe this deluge of information is a factor to consider in the high levels of anxiety we are witnessing in our time, enhanced by COVID-19 and the stress of job insecurity and a lack of social interaction during the pandemic.

The UK Chief Medical Officer has estimated that the wider costs of mental health problems to the UK economy are £70-£100 billion per year – 4.5 per cent of gross domestic product (GDP). Globally, more than 300 million people suffer from depression, which has become the leading cause of disability. More than 260 million are living with anxiety disorders. Many of these people live with both. A recent WHO-led study estimates that depression and anxiety disorders cost the global economy US$1 trillion each year in lost productivity.

Business can play its part in creating a more benevolent environment that allows us all to achieve our potential… and is compassionate when we cannot do so.

190. Making money is very difficult – but losing it is easy.

This is probably the most important point I have learned about money.

Some 25 years ago, I lost a seven-figure sum when my shares crashed. It was a bitter price to pay for a lifetime of hard work and, after a serious breakdown, I checked into the Priory Hospital. After treatment and care I plunged back into the corporate world and, fortunately, I never lost my perseverance and nose for business. But it has made me very conscious of the stress facing so many in our frenetic modern world.

191. The six best doctors in the world are: sunlight, rest, exercise, diet, self-confidence and friends.

Steve Jobs, Apple founder

This advice is valid for your entire life!

192. An annual medical check-up is a sound investment.

On the basis that prevention is better than cure, a good medical check-up will pick up any concerns that may need to be investigated.

Looking after your body will in turn help look after your mind.

193. Sitting all day at a computer is the new smoking – and your health is your wealth.

Sitting all day at a computer is the new smoking – and your health is your wealth.

Incorporate plenty of movement into your working day. Use lunchtime to go for a walk and get up out of your chair every 30 minutes or so to avoid potentially debilitating neck and back problems.

If possible, be disciplined to do some exercise every day. Ideally the morning is best because it is amazing how often something crops up that replaces your best intentions to exercise.

194. Rules for happiness: something to do, someone to love, something to hope for.

Immanuel Kant, German philosopher

195. Nothing is permanent in this world, not even our troubles.

In the UK, one in four people suffer from serious stress or mental health problems. There is nothing to be ashamed of. Recognize it, lift the lid and seek support from family, friends and professionals as needed.

Practising gratitude and implementing this practice into our daily lives starts with the smallest actions: being thankful for a morning coffee, kindly greeting a stranger with hello, and paying attention to how good it feels to experience the return of a simple smile.

I have gained immense support from my work as president of Shawmind, a charity that raises awareness of the importance of mental health in children, schools and the workplace. Seeing the difference we are making in transforming lives is an absolute joy. You can learn more about the charity and its ongoing efforts at www. shawmind.org.

196. The most wasted day in life is the day in which we have not laughed.

197. There is no pillow so soft as a clear conscience.

French proverb

Sleep is a crucial component to being effective in business. Whilst there are always exceptions, such as Margaret Thatcher, who boasted she needed only four hours a night, plenty of sleep is vital to making good investment or career decisions.

Too little sleep, like too much alcohol, can be dangerous.

198. People will forget what you said, people will forget what you did, but people will never forget how you made them feel.

Maya Angelou, poet, memoirist and civil rights activist

199. It's essential we all look after our own mental health.

I once had a boss who regarded me as a threat to his career and found fault with all I did. Although I kept up a strong front, I suffered emotionally and therefore paid a high price for staying at the company.

We need to check in with people if we think they are struggling, especially having learned so much about mental health during COVID-19.

200. Working from home can be both good and bad. If you never switch off, you face the danger of burnout.

Too many worry, "What if I miss something crucial?", escalating to, "What if I lose my job?" etc.

It is essential to keep life in balance.

201. Today you could be standing next to someone who is trying their best not to fall apart. So, whatever you do today, do it with kindness in your heart.

202. There's power in a simple hug.

Sometimes the worst place you can be is in your own head. Sometimes in life, you just need a hug. No words, no advice, just a hug to make you feel better.

203. As you climb the corporate ladder, never forget the importance of family balance.

Family

Health

Friends

Enough Money

As you climb the corporate ladder, never forget the importance of family balance.

Family, friends, health and enough money to enjoy the other three.

204. Live in the present moment. The past is history, the future a mystery and today is a gift, that's why it's called the present.
Eleanor Roosevelt, former First Lady of the United States

205. When our emotional health is poor, so is our self-esteem. It's time to slow down and deal with what is troubling us so that we can enjoy the simple joy of being happy and at peace with ourselves.
Jess C. Scott, author and artist

206. Spend 30 minutes in nature every day. Unless you're too busy, then you should spend an hour.

207. Almost everything will work again if you unplug it for a few minutes... including you.
Anne Lammott, quoted in Country Living

208. Too often we underestimate the power of a touch, a smile, a kind word, a listening ear, an honest compliment or the smallest act of caring, all of which have the potential to turn a life around.
Leo Buscaglia, American professor and motivational speaker

209. We are all broken in some way... but even broken crayons can fill a page with glorious colour.
Anonymous

If you have been feeling overwhelmed and stressed out a lot, it would be wise to rethink and rework your priorities. The simple truth is that "I can do anything, but not everything".

Free yourself up to pursue what really matters. More effort does not necessarily yield more results. "Less but better" does.

---

210. The secret of long life is to be optimistic and believe things can only get better.

Captain Sir Tom Moore, who lived to be 100 and raised more than £30 million for the NHS during lockdown

---

CHAPTER 13
RESILIENCE

The World Health Organization describes stress as the "global health epidemic of the 21st century." Work cultures are often constantly connected and highly demanding, fuelling stress and burnout. It's easy to feel overwhelmed by uncertainty without having the head space to think ahead. Resilience is a crucial part of coping with the emotional demands of these difficult times.

211. Finish each day and be done with it.

Ralph Waldo Emerson, American essayist and philosopher

You have done what you could. Yes, you made a few mistakes, but learn from them or forget them as soon as you can. Tomorrow is a new day; begin it well and in good spirits.

212. When life hands you a lemon, try to turn it into a margarita.

When life hands you a lemon, try to turn it into a margarita.

213. Sometimes life blossoms not despite a troubled childhood, but because of the tough times growing up.

I know from my own experience that had my father been rich, I would probably never have got a degree or had the motivation to succeed.

Growing up, money was very tight, and I spent ten and a half years at boarding school as one of the poorer kids. I went home twice a year from Cape Town to Zambia and only saw my parents for a few weeks at a time. Boarding school was not easy – showing emotion was taken as a sign of weakness, and I was surrounded by pupils flaunting their money, which I regarded as flashy and careless – but it gave me the drive to make something of my life.

214. The ultimate measure of a person is not where they sit in moments of comfort, but where they stand in times of challenge and controversy.

215. If at first you don't succeed, try, try and try again.

Persistence and going the extra mile are often vital in life. There are always hurdles, barriers and problems that must be accepted but do not have to defeat you. They are obstacles to be overcome.

James Dyson tested 5,126 prototypes before he got his vacuum cleaner right. J.K. Rowling was told not to quit her day job by a publisher, and the first *Harry Potter* novel was rejected 12 times. In 1962 a Decca record executive told The Beatles, "You have no future in show business."

So, while it is very easy to become disheartened and demotivated as time goes by, you have to remind yourself why you set your goals in the first place. That is key to making sure you are going to get there.

216. It is not the strongest of the species that survive, nor the most intelligent, but the one most responsive to change.

Charles Darwin, naturalist and founder of modern evolutionary studies

217. Viruses are contagious; so is panic, fear and hysteria. But so are calm, love, enthusiasm, kindness and joy. Choose wisely.

Dr. Caroline Leaf, neuroscientist

218. If you feel burnout setting in, if you feel demoralized and exhausted, it is best for the sake of everyone to withdraw and restore yourself. The point is to have a long-term perspective.

The Dalai Lama, the highest spiritual leader of Tibet

219. There is nothing wrong in admitting you do not know.

And more important – at times admitting you were wrong.

220. If you are suffering from anxiety, don't bottle it up.

Do not be embarrassed to seek support. Sharing will help both physically and mentally.

221. Criticism may not be agreeable, but it is necessary. It fulfils the same function as pain in the human body. It calls attention to an unhealthy state of things.

Winston Churchill

222. Any fool can criticize, condemn and complain, but it takes character and self-control to be understanding and forgiving.

Norman Vincent Peale, author of The Power of Positive Thinking

223. People have a right to their opinion, and you have a right to ignore it.

People have a right to their opinion, and you have a right to ignore it.

224. Learn to laugh at yourself before you laugh at others.

We are all human and we all make mistakes.

225. There is no such thing as 100 per cent perfect, it does not exist – simply do the best you can.

If you understand this, there is no need to flagellate yourself pointlessly. Very rarely do we get everything right, and the key is to be willing to make corrections during life's journey.

226. Don't spend your life being envious of other people.

Jealousy and envy are dangerous sources of unhappiness. Things are not always what they seem, very much including other people. Spend your time focusing on the good things in your own life and what you can hopefully do to make things even better.

227. Without exception we all need to find balance in our lives.

Here are five rules for a good life:

1. Eat well
2. Avoid stress where possible
3. Be part of a community
4. Stay active
5. And have a sense of purpose.

228. As you go about your life, find a balance between pleasure and purpose and always make time to think.

Take a moment to pause and remember who you truly are. Reflect on the things that have real and lasting meaning in your life. This will better help you get your business and personal life in balance.

Also remember that when juggling home and work, perfection in everything is impossible – so do not waste energy feeling guilty.

229. In life you always need a balance between mental and physical activity.

And you should never stop learning – whether it's a new business skill, taking up a sport you've never tried before, a foreign language, cooking or gardening.

230. How many people on their deathbed wish they had spent more time in the office?

Stephen Covey, author of First Things First

CHAPTER 14
RESPECT AND FRIENDSHIP

231. Kindness is a language that the blind can see and the deaf can hear.

Coronavirus stressed the magic of kindness – it is a gentle breeze that touches everybody.

232. Weigh your words as carefully as if they were gold dust.

Words are the most potent force we have. We can use them constructively, offering words of encouragement, or destructively, scattering words that demean. They possess energy and strength, with the ability to help, heal... or to hinder, hurt, harm, humiliate and humble.

233. A definition of respect today is to put your phone away in every meeting and at every meal to pay attention to those talking to you.

234. When I want your opinion, I will give it to you.

Samuel Goldwyn, film producer

These words were once repeated by my boss. I knew my days in that business were numbered. He obviously didn't respect me – and he was someone I didn't want to work for.

235. In today's electronic world, a handwritten note of thanks or appreciation really means something.

236. Life is fraught with opportunities to keep your mouth shut.

Winston Churchill

Life is fraught with opportunities to keep your mouth shut.

237. There are negative spin doctors everywhere, not just in 10 Downing Street!

Remember that telling someone something in confidence means that they will only tell one person at a time.

Beware who you confide in. If you voice negative thoughts, do so in the knowledge that they will soon be buzzing all around the office. Gossiping about your co-workers will only reflect badly on you.

238. I don't trust anyone who is nice to me but rude to the waiter. How would they treat me if I were in the same position?

Muhammad Ali, boxing superstar

Treat all people, no matter how junior, with respect. As a leader, remain calm, pleasant and rational, and involve your team constructively in problem solving. Never scream or shout in the office because all you do is damage morale, productivity… and your own reputation.

239. Resentment is like drinking poison, then hoping it will kill your enemies.

240. A sweet friendship refreshes the soul.

Proverbs 27:9

241. One good friend is equal to one good medicine. One good group is equal to one full pharmacy.

As life rolls on, we realize it is less important to have lots of friends and more important to have real ones. In the business world you only discover who are your real friends when you leave the business.

Sadly, in the business world, there are too many people with big egos who, in the end, are ruined by praise from sycophantic ambitious underlings! Be careful.

242. It is the privilege of friendship to talk nonsense and to have the nonsense respected.

Charles Lamb, 18th-century English essayist

243. Wishing to be friends is quick work, but friendship is like a slow-ripening fruit.

Aristotle, ancient Greek philosopher

244. Good friends are the real jewels of life – difficult to find and impossible to replace.

Anonymous

And you probably won't find many of them at work. When I lost my job (on my wedding anniversary, as it happened), I was fascinated and saddened to see who among my friends in the office called and who didn't.

245. Keep your office out of the bedroom, especially because modern life with its all-pervasive technology is stressful enough.

Keep your office out of the bedroom.

246. Never ignore a person who loves you, cares for you and misses you. Because one day, you might wake up from your sleep and realize that you lost the moon while counting the stars.
Nico Lang, essayist, critic and national LGBTQ+ reporter

247. A true friend is someone who thinks you are a good egg, even though they know you are slightly cracked.
Bernard Meltzer, American radio host

248. One of the secrets of life is that all that is really worth doing, is what we do for others.
Lewis Carroll, author

249. Anything is possible when you have the right people to support you.

Misty Copeland, American ballet dancer

250. Value people you have known for a long time because they know your past – and it doesn't matter.

251. Success can easily breed arrogance and forgetting the value of old friends – beware.

True friendship is not about what you get but what you are able to give, so always have time for old and new friends in life.

CHAPTER 15
SOUND PERSONAL FINANCE

252. Don't panic about short-term dips.

A good personal investment plan helps you to stay calm in almost all circumstances, and COVID-19 certainly put that to the test. One of the most important qualities for any investor is a good temperament and patience.

In tough times people panic too easily. Patience is not simply the ability to wait, but how we behave while we are nervously waiting.

253. Be very cautious about "sure-thing" investments. There is no such thing.

254. When you lend someone money, regard it as a bonus if you get it back.

When you lend someone money, regard it as a bonus if you get it back.

255. Don't be greedy.

There is no such thing as the top of the market. It is wise to take some profit intelligently on at least a section of your investment.

256. You cannot win the lottery if you don't buy a ticket.

257. Don't invest in things you don't understand.

Warren Buffett, billionaire investor and philanthropist

258. Ideally invest for the long term.

Good, solid investments suggest taking a sound long-term view using the best possible advice available. Only speculate with money you can afford to lose. If you invest in start-ups, you must have extreme patience. I believe and have always stated publicly that it takes ten years to build a decent brand. Never forget that most new brands fail.

You do not want to waste money, but you do want to invest wisely and steadily. If you do not have the necessary skillset yourself, make sure you choose recommended and approved advisers or investment firms to help you make the best decisions.

259. Watch the pounds and the pennies don't matter.

I prefer this mantra to the usual: "Watch the pennies and the pounds will look after themselves."

260. If anything looks to be too good to be true, it probably is.

When it comes to investments and pensions, be very wary of unexpected and unlikely offers.

261. There is one iron-clad rule in history: the law of unintended consequences.

Nothing is ever guaranteed. From a supposed "hot tip" on the stock market to getting a win with your premium bonds!

262. Always borrow money from a pessimist because at least you know they won't expect it back.

Oscar Wilde, playwright

Alternatively...

263. Pay what you owe, and you will know what you own.

Benjamin Franklin

264. Whilst it is important to be measured and take a long-term view with investments, the biggest risk of all is not to take one.

265. If you have made money, do not put all your eggs in one basket.

Diversify your portfolio: pension, property, shares, cash and hopefully also lots of money for worthy causes.

PART 4
LEADERSHIP

CHAPTER 16
HOW TO DEVELOP LEADERSHIP QUALITIES

266. The essence of leadership is that while managers have subordinates, leaders have followers.

Roger Gill, Director *magazine*

You are appointed a manager but only become a leader when your appointment is ratified in the hearts and minds of those working around you.

267. An orchestra without a conductor is only a room full of musicians and instruments.

An orchestra without a conductor is only a room full of musicians and instruments.

Management is simply getting things done — it is leadership that gives direction and sets the course.

268. Nearly all people can stand adversity, but if you want to test a person's character, give them power.

Adapted from Abraham Lincoln, former US President

269. A leader is like a shepherd. He stays behind the flock, letting the most nimble go out ahead, whereupon the others follow, not realizing that all along they are being directed from behind.

Nelson Mandela, former South African President, world statesman, freedom fighter and political prisoner

270. No man will be a great leader who wants to do it all himself, or to get all the credit for doing it.

Andrew Carnegie, Scottish-American industrialist and philanthropist

271. The first responsibility of a leader is to define reality. The last is to say, "Thank you." In between, the leader is a servant.

Max de Pree, American businessman

272. We should all learn from good horse management. The more you use the reins, the less a horse uses its brain.

273. Climb the mountain so you can see the world, not so the world can see you.

David McCullough Jr., teacher

Be humble. The best leaders are content not to be the smartest person in the room or the one with all the answers. Surround yourself with capable experts and be prepared to listen to them.

274. Always have an open door to listen to your team's personal problems.

You may be a strong leader, but you must also be compassionate.

275. The man who knows how will always have the job. The man who also knows why will always be his boss.

Ralph Waldo Emerson

276. A good leader inspires men to have confidence in him. A great leader inspires them to have confidence in themselves.

Lao Tzu, ancient Chinese philosopher

277. Leadership is cultivated, not wished into being.

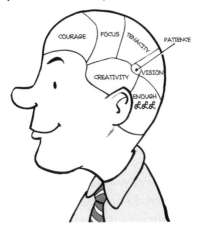

Do you have what it takes?

If you want to manage others successfully, you have to manage yourself by developing a consistent decision-making and leadership style that everyone in the company understands.

278. Leadership is about having the courage to make decisions coupled with the humility to listen.

279. Asking for help is a sign of a confident leader.

It shows people you trust them, that you value their opinions and that you all share the same goals for the success of the business.

280. Whilst it is good to be an optimist, as a leader never over-promise and under-deliver.

281. The chief executive of the future must be an inclusive leader who gives staff a voice and is no longer a traditional command-and-control operator.

Someone who leads, not dictates… who delegates, motivates and inspires.

282. Joining a board is not a reward in itself, but the beginning of shared responsibility.

Your day job may be functional, but your directorship is for the good of the total business.

283. In business and life, you don't have to know everything that is going on – you need to understand what is relevant.

284. The leader is one who, out of the clutter, brings simplicity… out of discord, harmony… and out of difficulty, opportunity.

Albert Einstein

CHAPTER 17
ACT LIKE A LEADER

285. The few who do are the envy of the many who only watch.

Jim Rohn, American entrepreneur and author

286. More than ever in our rapidly shrinking world, great leaders make history and not the other way around.

In periods where there is no leadership, or when there is warped leadership, society stands still.

Progress occurs when courageous, skilful leaders seize the opportunity to change things for the better.

287. Leaders who don't listen will eventually find themselves surrounded by people who have nothing to say.

288. Always hire people who are smarter than you.

They may be challenging sometimes, but they are far better than "yes men".

And…

289. I'm not the smartest fellow in the world, but I can sure pick smart colleagues.

Franklin D. Roosevelt, former US President

290. Good managers do not hide in their offices.

Good managers do not hide in their offices.

Make a point of being visible, talk to people from all aspects of your business, and spend time in the marketplace meeting real customers.

291. Simplify, decentralize management and incentivize people running the business at the divisional level.

David Roper, former CEO of Melrose plc, a FTSE 100 company that specializes in buying and improving underperforming businesses

292. In tough times, great leaders communicate openly and often with their teams.

They face bad news head-on and tell their people the truth.

293. If you want the co-operation of humans around you, you must make them feel they are important – and you do this by being genuine and humble.

Nelson Mandela

294. Meetings are cul-de-sacs down which creative ideas are often lured and then quietly strangled.

Sir Thomas Barnett Cocks, former Clerk of the House of Commons

Good leaders recognize this and ensure that meetings are structured, focused and relevant.

295. Be the last to speak.
This is the mantra of my friend Derek Wilson, a leadership coach, who recommends using it in meetings to empower people.

While the logic behind the idea is unassailable, putting the wisdom into practice can be harder than it sounds. We are all dying to jump in and prove our brilliance, push our own ideas or correct others' errors.

If you can manage to keep your mouth shut, you will instantly level up your leadership – so listening will make you smarter.

---

296. The chief executive of an organization is also the chief culture officer.

He or she sets the tone and is responsible for the wellbeing of the major asset of every company – its people.

From my experience, telling people what I intended to do and why, forced me to make a commitment and ensured that I followed through. It is often a useful bit of constructive pressure.

A good, caring chief executive, along with the chair of the board, creates a positive, inclusive culture to the benefit of all. A good culture and thus improved wellbeing leads to less absenteeism, less presenteeism, less staff turnover and greater productivity for the company... a win-win situation.

---

297. Before you are a leader, success is all about growing yourself. When you become a leader, success is all about growing others.
Jack Welch, former chairman and CEO of General Electric

Jack was so highly valued he received severance pay of $417 million on retirement!

298. Bad leadership is like a flat tyre. It is very hard to go anywhere until you change it.

299. Constructive delegation is a crucial part of being a good leader and team building.

Why keep a dog and bark yourself?

300. All proposals are welcome, as long as they are constructive and seek to improve.

Proposals should be encouraged but not if they just criticize someone else's idea. Instead, people should offer suggestions for how things might work better. This is a good method to stop them sniping at others and puts the onus on them to come up with an improvement.

301. Diplomacy is the art of telling people to go to hell in such a way that they ask for directions.

Winston Churchill

302. Being an NED is not a spectator sport.

A good board needs a mix of skills and personalities and an orderly transition of both executives and non-executives. Whilst a non-executive director (NED) is not actually a player, he or she is equally not a spectator. Besides legal responsibilities, a good non-exec should be creatively engaged and should also use shoe leather to view the operations and meet a variety of people in the company. Purely pitching up for meetings, having read the papers the night before, is not acceptable.

303. Effective chairs focus strongly on strategy, people and cash management.

While the chief executive manages the company and delivers the results, the chair manages the board and focuses on the strategy, key people and cash flow. Running the board includes shaping the agenda, which can significantly affect the business.

304. You know you're no longer chairman when you sit in the back of the car and it does not move.

...When you sit in the back of the car and it does not move.

Do not become arrogant because of your position. A title is temporary, and things can change in a heartbeat.

PART 5
ENTREPRENEURSHIP

CHAPTER 18
HOW TO DEVELOP AN ENTREPRENEURIAL MINDSET

305. Learning from failure is often the way to success.

Leaders should embrace an entrepreneurial mindset: be determined to find simple solutions and new ways to make things better, quickly. This can only happen if you create a culture that rewards risk-taking and forgives failures.

306. Working hard without purpose or focus is a recipe for undue stress. Working hard for something you love, fires you with passion and pride.

307. Just because you are a good cook, doesn't mean you should open a restaurant.

You'll need more than recipes – for example, a great experience to offer your customers, unique reasons for them to buy from you, a strong team and enough cash to see you through the undoubted hard times ahead.

308. The great inventors of the world very rarely worked alone.

Most had a hidden team of colleagues and loved ones who helped them.

Albert Einstein struggled before his former classmate Michele Besso helped him crack the theory of relativity. Likewise, Alexander

Fleming discovered penicillin by accident after a dish of bacteria went mouldy – but it took a team of Oxford scientists to work out how to purify penicillin and turn it into the amazing drug we know today.

309. Genius is one per cent inspiration, ninety-nine per cent perspiration.
Thomas Edison, inventor

310. It always seems impossible – until it is done.
Nelson Mandela

311. I am not going to tell you the road ahead will be easy, but I will tell you that you have the power to keep walking one step at a time toward a better future – the choice is yours.

312. One man with conviction will overwhelm a hundred who have only opinions.
Winston Churchill

313. Whenever you see a successful business, someone once made a courageous decision.

Professor Peter Drucker

314. Can you last the journey?
With any new brand or business, breaking even usually takes twice as long and twice as much money as you ever thought. Also remember that fundamental requirements of entrepreneurship are courage, tenacity and cash management.

315. The road ahead is always under construction, but you have to go the extra mile – and if you ain't the lead dog, the scenery never changes.

Edmund Wilson, American critic

316. When you leave corporate life to go out on your own, leave your big-company mentality behind you.

Enjoy being top dog, but don't become arrogant!

317. The world is moving so fast these days that the person who says it can't be done is generally interrupted by someone doing it.

Elbert Hubbard, American writer and philosopher

318. Honourable and great entrepreneurs share the glory and the rewards.

If you start your own company, ensure (in the early stages especially) that you hire outstanding people and all benefit if success is achieved.

CHAPTER 19
ACT LIKE AN ENTREPRENEUR

319. Every business should have a clear mission statement.

This is essential, especially if you are a start-up. It should set out your aims and thus help the team understand why they do what they do – and why they get up in the morning.

It will guide management's thinking on strategic issues, define performance standards, inspire employees to work more productively, provide focus and common goals, and establish a framework for ethical behaviour. As Bain & Company says, it also has external value, enlisting support and creating closer links and better communication with customers, suppliers and partners, as well as serving as a public relations tool.

In a nutshell, it helps to ensure the boat rows harmoniously in the right direction.

320. Stars cannot shine without darkness.

Do not give up too quickly – you will inevitably have to go many extra miles to reach your destination.

321. The harder you practise, the luckier you get.

Gary Player, great South African golfer

Make your own luck. In these tough times, earn success by consistently focusing on great service and small acts of kindness to bring in customers.

Of course, you need talent, but the difference between good and great is often a matter of dedication, commitment and application. In business, how hard you work and how well you work with people are the keys.

322. Who invented the wheel? Someone who thought it was possible.

Who invented the wheel? Someone who thought it was possible.

The 21st century is full of great challenges. Can you make the impossible – possible? Those who do are the true entrepreneurs and a lot of this will be in the technological space.

323. Logic will get you from A to B. Imagination will take you everywhere.
Albert Einstein

324. It is not the employer who pays the wages. Employers only handle the money. It is the customer who pays the wages.
Henry Ford, founder of Ford Motors

325. Know what business you are really in.
No, you don't sell water coolers, you sell better hydration for a healthier lifestyle! Truly understand your business and the benefits it brings.

326. The opportunity of a lifetime must be seized within the lifetime of the opportunity.

Leonard Ravenhill, English Christian evangelist

327. Hard work will never make a success of a venture if the basic idea is flawed.

So, be brutal in assessing how your venture can genuinely benefit society.

328. Don't trust everything you see... even salt looks like sugar.

329. Fame has many fathers, but failure is an orphan.

330. Be prepared to live frugally, make sacrifices and travel the cheapest way en route to the promised land.

Having chaired a large company with 6,000 staff, with the use of a chauffeur and flying first class, I launched my own company, The Last Drop Distillers Limited, aged 65 in 2008. I certainly put living frugally into practice!

331. Turnover is for vanity, profit is for sanity, but only cash is reality.

You can't bank turnover or profit, and many businesses fail, not because the product or business is bad, but because they have run out of cash.

332. The time to buy an umbrella is when it's not raining.

The time to negotiate an overdraft or financial facility is when you don't need it. If you do not, it will be very difficult and very expensive in a crisis – if you are able to negotiate anything at all.

333. There is no magic bullet.

In all but the very rarest of cases, there is no result without hard work.

334. The biggest risk is not taking any risk. In a world that is changing really quickly, the only strategy that is guaranteed to fail is not taking risks.

Mark Zuckerberg, founder of Facebook

The biggest risk is not taking any risk.

PART 6
WHAT NEXT?

CHAPTER 20

THE POST-COVID BUSINESS WORLD

As societies, economies and individuals, we have all gone through a life-changing shock as a result of COVID-19. Even before the coronavirus pandemic, we were already living in a world of ever-faster change, from automation and artificial intelligence to the need for fresh thinking to mitigate the perils of global warming.

There is much we can and must do to improve the global environment and the world in which we live.

335. The world needs huge positive energy to fight against the negative forces. Go to the centre of your inner being and generate that positive energy for the welfare of the humanity.
Amit Ray, author of World Peace: The Voice of a Mountain Bird

336. A sustainable business functions in the best interests of both the local and global environment – it considers its impact on society and the world around us.
Antonia Jamieson, British businesswoman

337. There are decades where nothing happens and there are weeks where decades happen.
Vladimir Lenin, leader of the 1917 Russian Revolution

338. These so-called bleak times are necessary to go through, in order to get to a much better place.

David Lynch, musician and film director

Sadly, as COVID-19 has shown us, we have to look seriously at the consequences of feeding the planet's increasing population, the dangers of global warming and rising sea levels if the future world is going to be a good place to live in.

Your role is to create a sustainable business that can play its part in helping to achieve the UN's ambitious Sustainable Development Goals.

339. Whilst many jobs in the future will be automated, you cannot automate creativity, empathy and innovation.

340. The COVID-19 pandemic will lead to permanent social, economic and cultural changes. The key is to create good from a bad situation.

Wayne Gerard Trotman, author and film director

341. In the post-COVID world, people have a different view of work and expect leaders to see them as human beings first and foremost.

Businesses that maintain a duty of care to employees, whatever the disruption, will be the ones that prosper in the long term.

342. Short-term financial greed is not good for the future of capitalism.

Since the turn of the century, we have seen too much avaricious behaviour from too many fast deals and excesses. This has to change to protect the future of good capitalism and to look after our precious globe for the future of mankind.

343. Your idea is great – I am glad I thought of it.

Good ideas are sometimes stolen, adapted, adopted.

A boss said this to me some 50 years ago. I was just starting out then, so I allowed him to *take* the credit. More than ever, however, I recognize the importance of *sharing* the credit when teamwork creates success!

344. In troubled times, small gestures of goodwill can make a big difference to individuals and society.

Help a neighbour or a colleague with a simple task, and engage strangers by chatting about the weather, dogs… anything. Some people go an entire day without speaking to anyone.

345. Learn to pivot like a pro.

Today's fast-paced world means business transformation will never be complete. You need the agility to adjust to changing threats and opportunities – combined with the calm reassurance to take people with you.

346. For many employees a return to pre-lockdown working practices is unacceptable and unthinkable.

Many staff expect more flexibility and the idea of working from home three days a week is more logical than many companies understand.

347. What you do makes a difference, and you have to decide what kind of difference you want to make.

Jane Goodall, the world's foremost expert on chimpanzees

CHAPTER 21
MONEY ISN'T EVERYTHING: THE VALUE
OF PHILANTHROPY

348. Making money is a means to an end – not an end in itself.
The more successful you become, the more important it is to have this in perspective. Giving back to society and using your wealth to help others are key to wellbeing – your mental wellbeing and the wellbeing of all those whose lives you can enhance.

349. If you are in the luckiest one per cent of humanity, you owe it to the rest of humanity to think about the other ninety-nine per cent.

Warren Buffett

350. I cannot believe the purpose of life is to be 'happy'. I think the purpose of life is to be useful, to be responsible, to be compassionate. It is, above all, to matter, to count, to stand for something, to have made some difference that you have lived at all.
Leo C. Rosten, American writer

351. Every moment spent impressing others leaves less time for doing good.

352. To plant a garden is to believe in tomorrow.
Audrey Hepburn, Hollywood actress

353. There are two ways to get enough. One is to continue to accumulate more and more. The other is to desire less.

G.K. Chesterton, writer and philosopher

354. The world won't change because you donate money, but it will change if your heart is changed. You can never save all the poor people and heal all the ills, but we can wake up the kindness inside everyone in the world.

Jack Ma, co-founder of multinational technology conglomerate Alibaba Group

When you have enough money for you and your family, think how you can best use the surplus to help society and those less fortunate.

355. Profit is a consequence of what you do well. It should never become a goal.

Bernard Arnault, billionaire businessman and art collector

Arnault is chairman and chief executive of Louis Vuitton Moët Hennessy, the world's largest luxury-goods company, so he knows a thing or two about profit.

356. There is no point in being the richest man in the cemetery.

Colonel Sanders, founder of Kentucky Fried Chicken

There is no point in being the richest man in the cemetery.

357. Giving and helping others is a reward in itself.

Do try to embrace this and contribute to the welfare of our troubled society.

358. No act of kindness, no matter how small, is ever wasted.

Aesop, ancient Greek storyteller

359. Success is getting what you want, but happiness is being content with what you get.

Life in true perspective should not be about getting and having, but rather about giving and being rewarded thereby.

Real wealth is achieved by being grateful for what you already have in your life.

360. If there was nothing wrong in the world, there wouldn't be anything for us to do.

George Bernard Shaw

361. You aren't wealthy until you have something money can't buy.

Garth Brooks, American singer and songwriter

Material benefits are helpful but true wealth comes from peace, contentment and happiness.

362. Wise entrepreneurs actively support the community in which they operate.

I know a local entrepreneur who has built up a great company over three decades, in large part because he is an avid supporter of local events and is hugely respected in our community – where his brand name is prominently displayed at all sorts of activities. The best thing about corporate social responsibility is that, when done properly, it should work for both the causes you support and your bottom line.

363. There are three key stages in life: Learn, Earn and Return.

Whilst you should never stop learning, the first phase of your life is about education. The second phase is about earning and looking after your family. As you move toward retirement, think about what you can do to give back to society and make it a better world for all.

364. Too many people who retire too quickly become complacent.

You may have made enough money to retire by the time you're 50 but think of everything you can still do in this world! Remain active and you'll find that helping people is also good for your health.

And finally... 365.

Sometime when you're feeling important,
Sometime when your ego's in bloom,
Sometime when you take it for granted
You're the best qualified in the room.
Sometime when you feel that your going
Would leave an unfillable hole,
Just follow this simple example
And see how it humbles your soul.
Take a bucket and fill it with water.
Put your hand in it up to your wrist.
Pull it out, and the hole that's remaining
Is a measure of how you'll be missed.
You may splash all you please when you enter
And stir up the water galore.
But stop, and you'll see in a minute
That it looks just the same as before.
The moral in this quaint example is
Do just the best that you can.

Be proud of yourself, but remember
There's no indispensable woman or man.
Anonymous

ACKNOWLEDGEMENTS

That this book of quotes has finally come to fruition is down to exceptional support from a number of my friends.

In particular I want to thank Derek Wilson, whom I have known for some 60 years and who spent a wonderful amount of time discussing quotes with me, sharing his ideas and proofreading. Thank you, Derek.

I am also indebted to my secretary and friend Christine Holland, who has put up with me for 22 years now. Her patient drafting, support and correction as and when required have been outstanding.

I also want to thank my editor, my friend Lesley Hussell of Editing Edge, who has diligently taken what I have scribbled and guided me to a perfectly structured form. Along with talented illustrator Cris Black and the Leaping Cow team, they have made the book come together in a hopefully fun and positive manner.

Last but not least, I owe a huge debt of gratitude to my wife Celia and our daughters Caroline and Jessica for their extreme patience and acceptance of the many hours I have spent muttering and hiding in my office.

ABOUT CHERISH EDITIONS

Cherish Editions is a bespoke author-funded publishing service for mental health, wellbeing and inspirational books.

As a division of the TriggerHub Group, the UK's leading independent mental health and wellbeing organization, we are experienced in creating and selling positive, responsible, important and inspirational pieces of bibliotherapy. Our books harness the power of a person's lived experience to guide others through their own mental health journeys and kick-start their recovery. We also work to de-stigmatize the issues around mental health and improve the wellbeing of those who read our titles.

Founded by Adam Shaw, a mental health advocate, author and philanthropist, and leading psychologist Lauren Callaghan, Cherish Editions aims to publish books that provide advice, support and inspiration. We nurture our authors so that their stories can unfurl on the page, helping them to share their uplifting and moving stories.

Cherish Editions is unique in that a percentage of the profits from the sale of our books goes directly to leading mental health charity Shawmind, to deliver its vision to provide support for those experiencing mental ill health.

Find out more about Cherish Editions by visiting cherisheditions.com or by joining us on:

Twitter @cherisheditions
Facebook @cherisheditions
Instagram @cherisheditions

Cherish
EDITIONS

ABOUT SHAWMIND

A proportion of profits from the sale of all Trigger books go to their sister charity Shawmind, also founded by Adam Shaw and Lauren Callaghan. The charity aims to ensure that everyone has access to mental health resources whenever they need them.

You can find out more about the work Shawmind do by visiting shawmind.org or joining them on:

Twitter @Shawmind_

Facebook @ShawmindUK

Instagram @Shawmind_

Your Local Mental Health & Wellbeing Charity

9 781913 615604